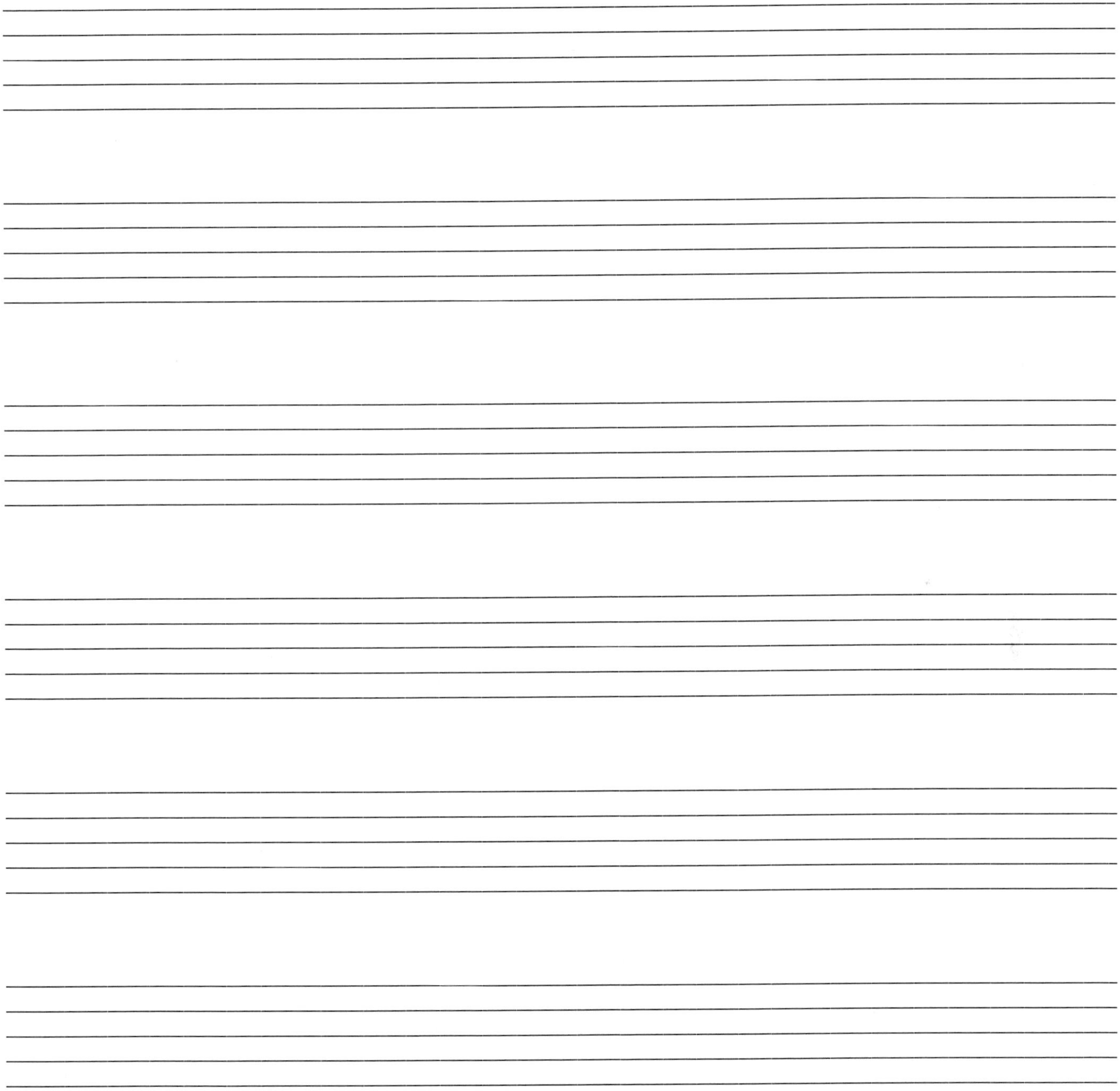

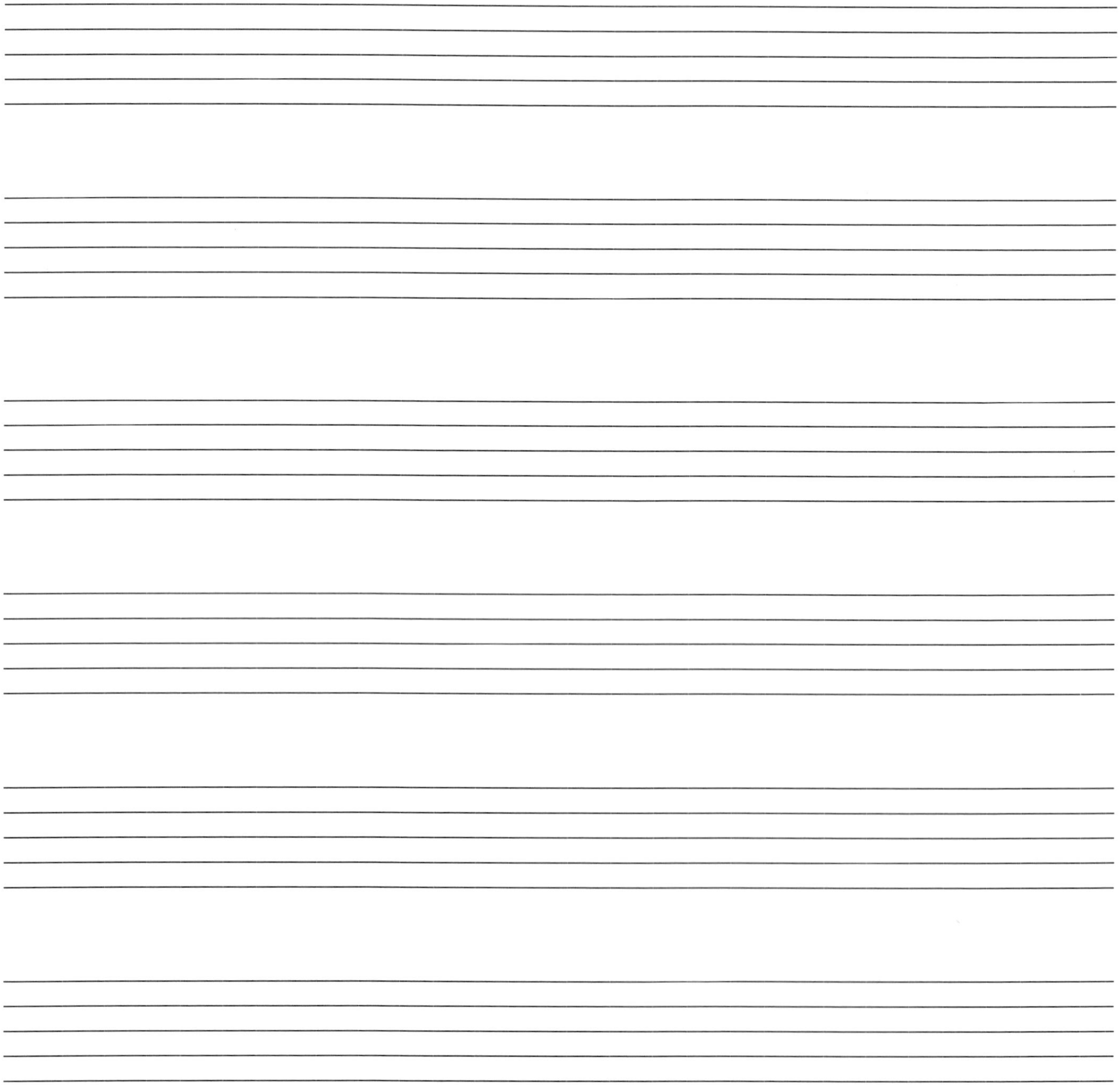

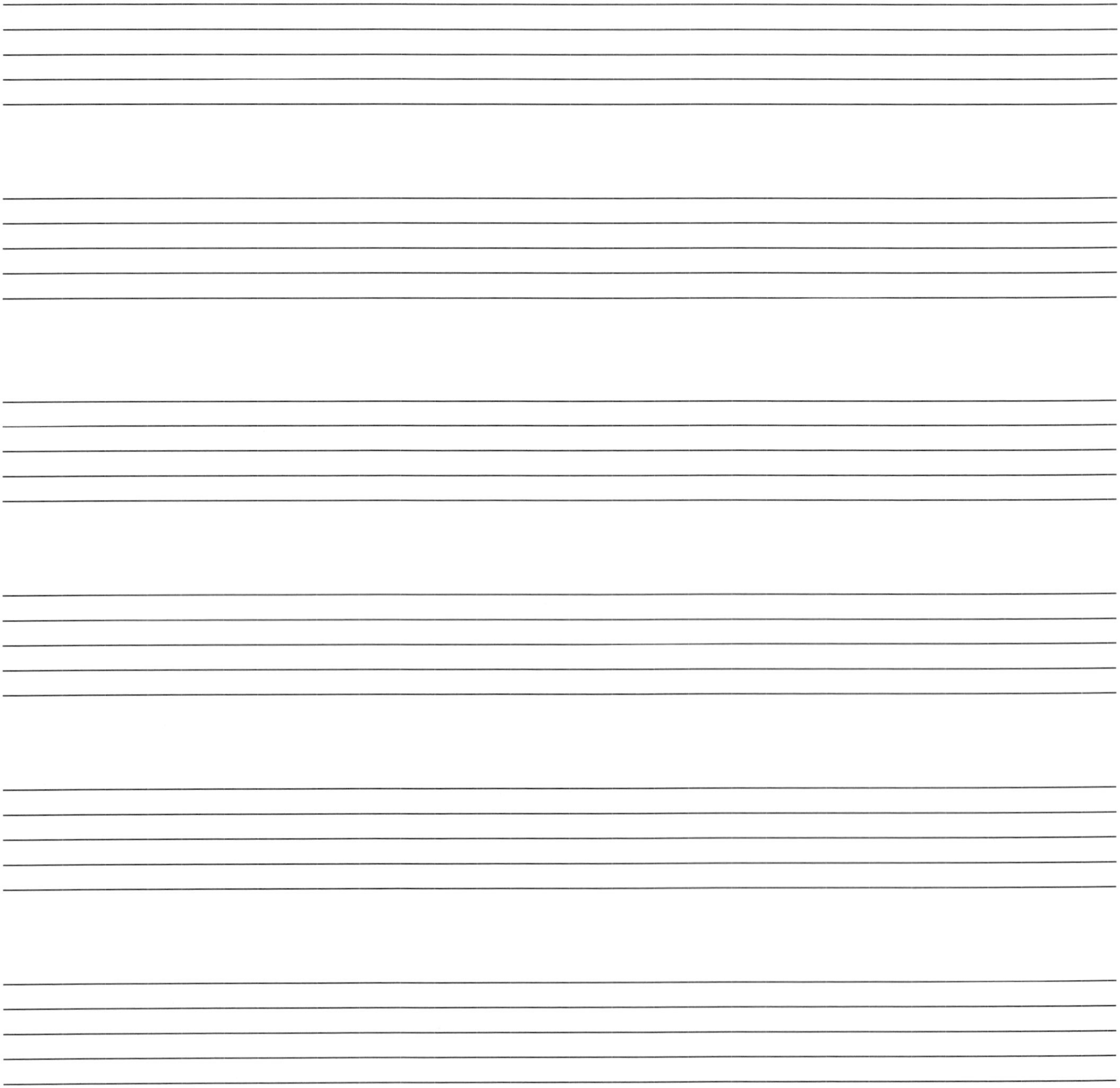

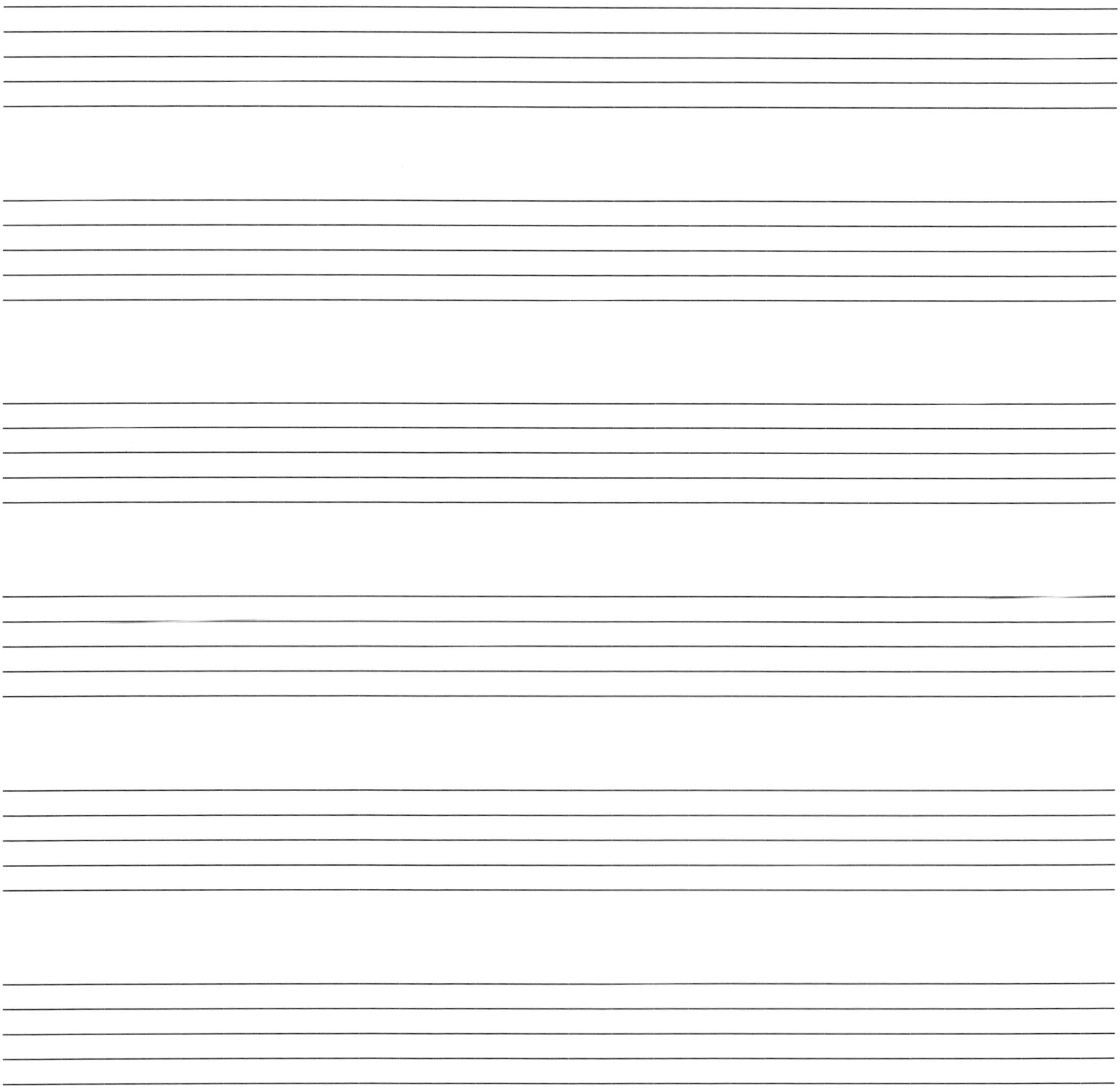

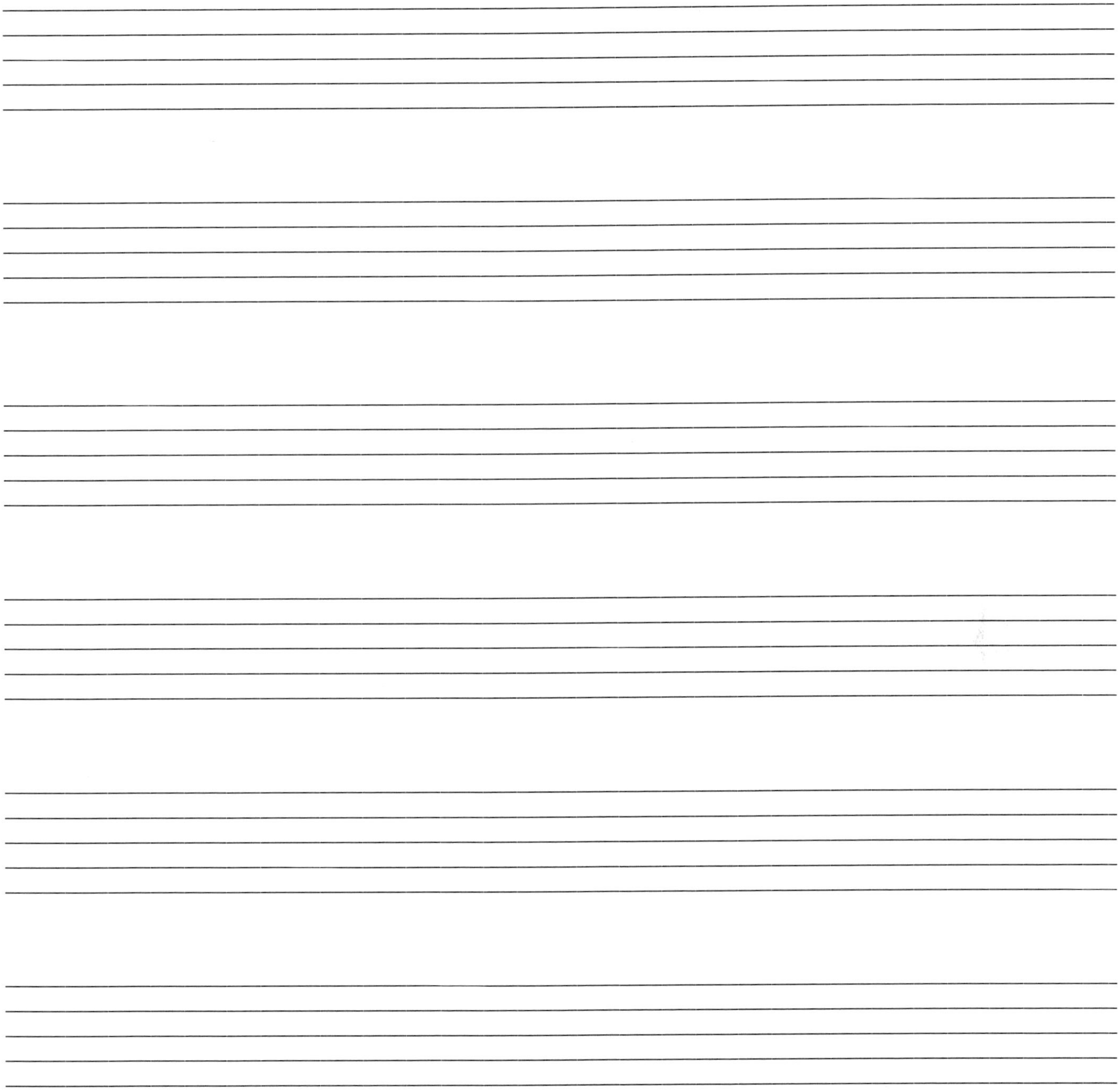

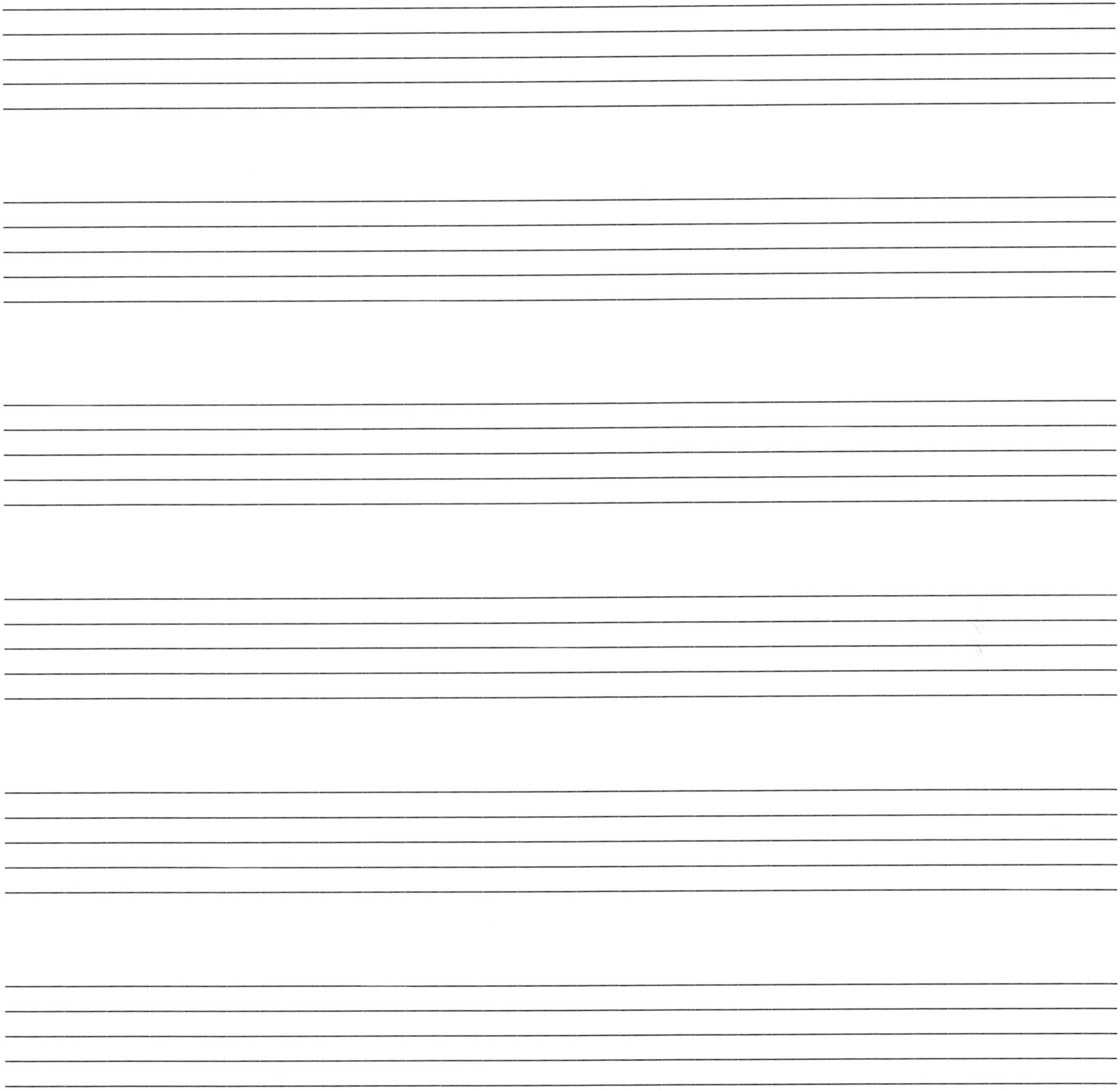

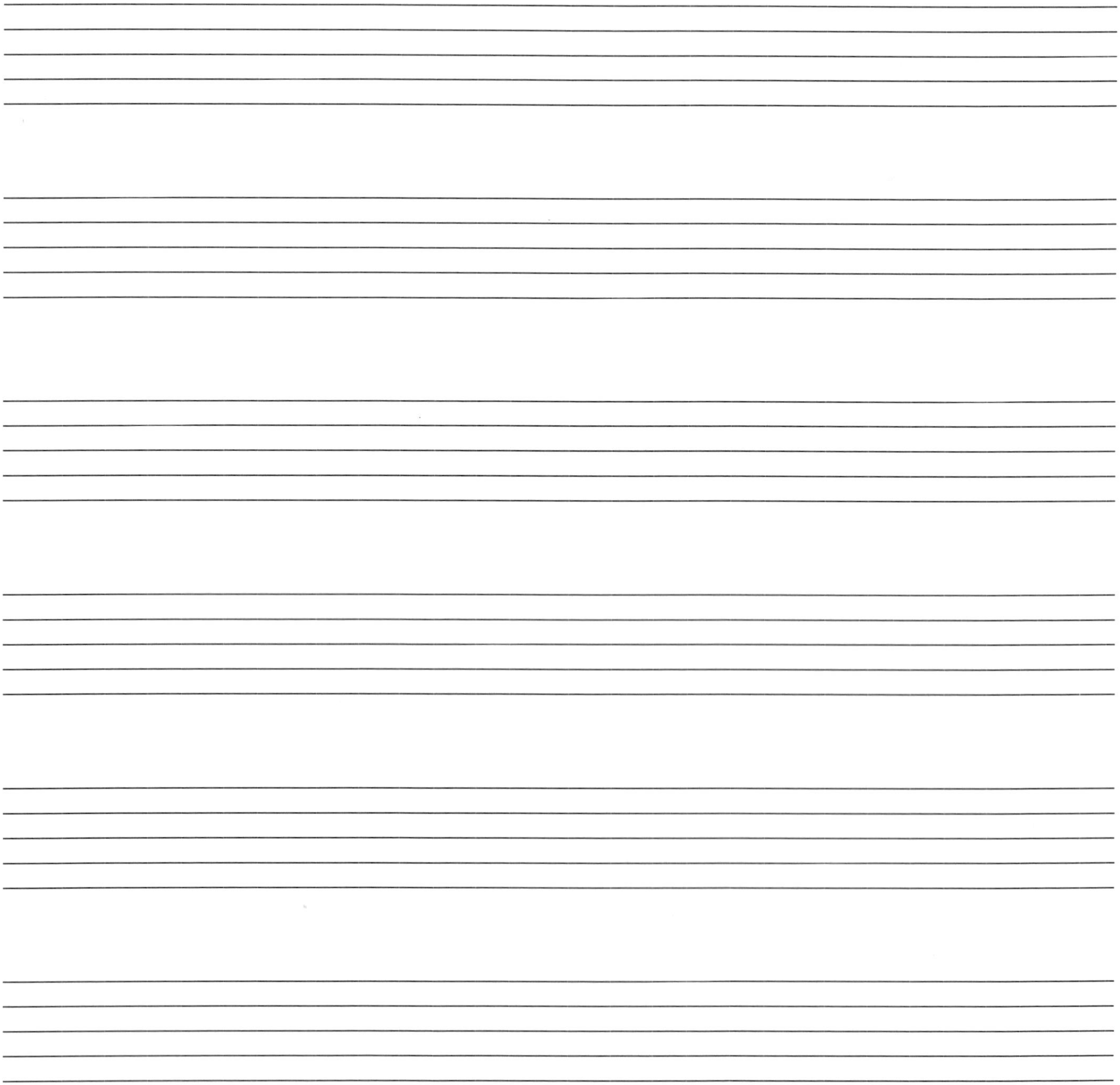

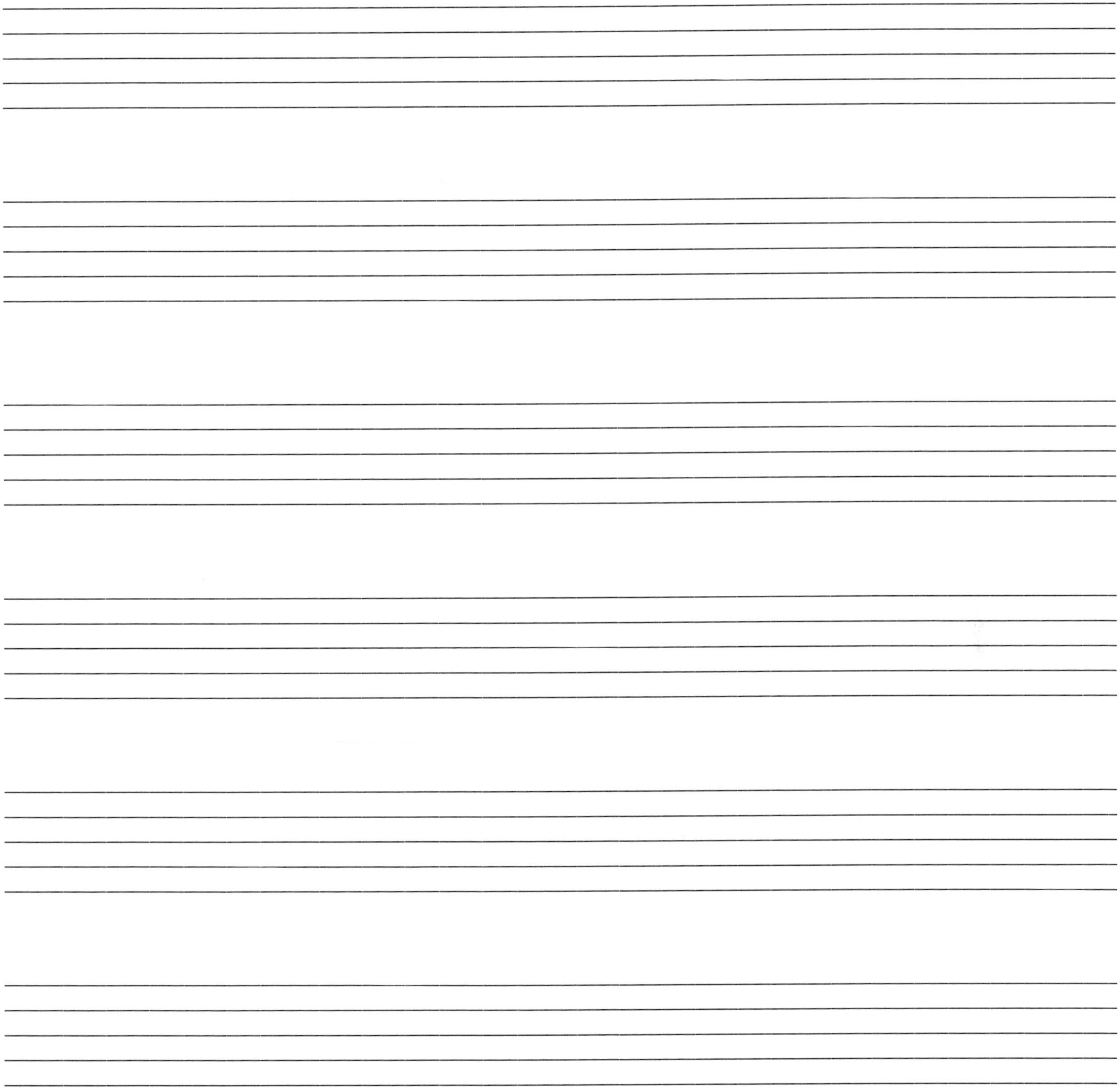

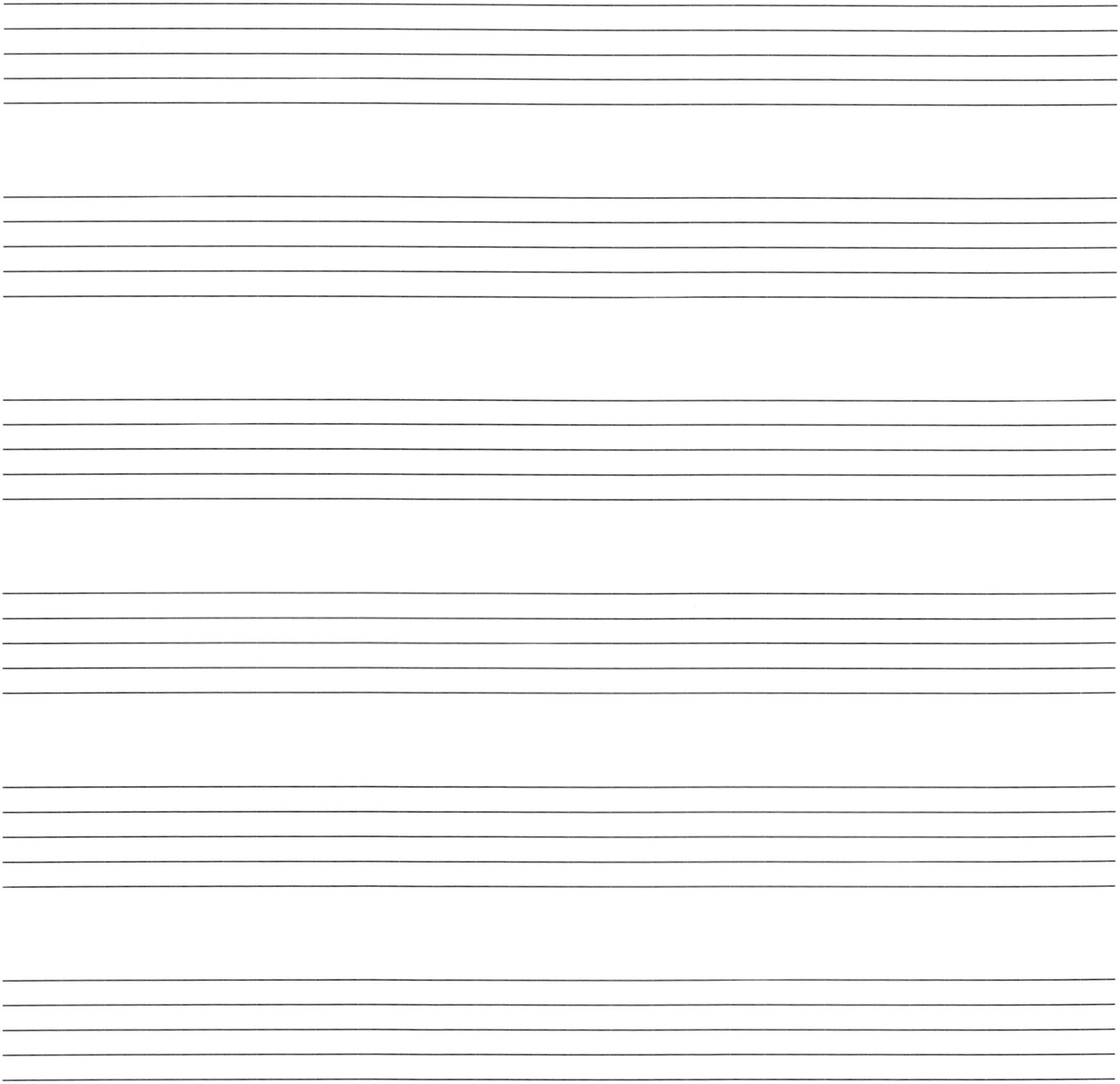

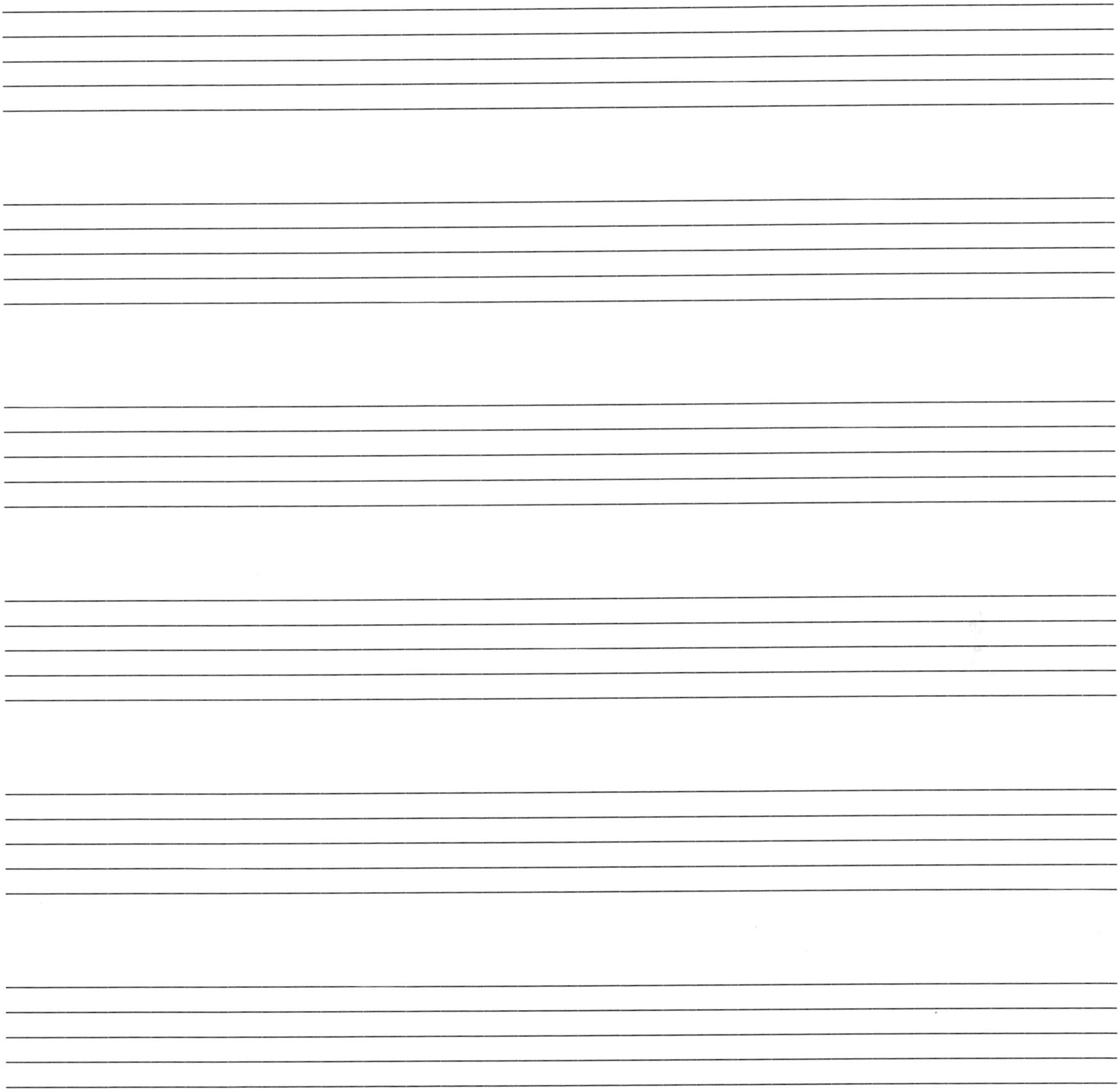

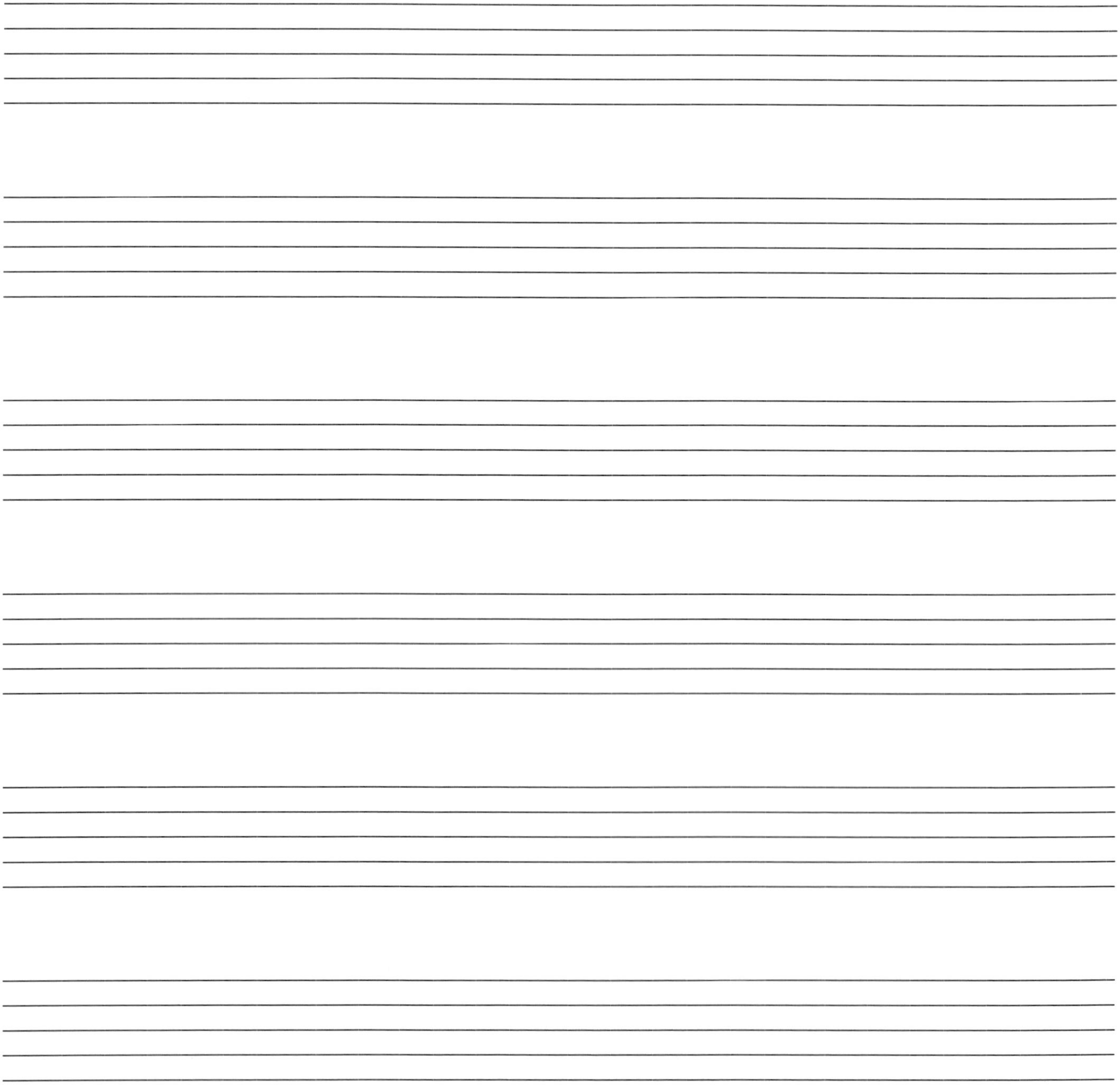

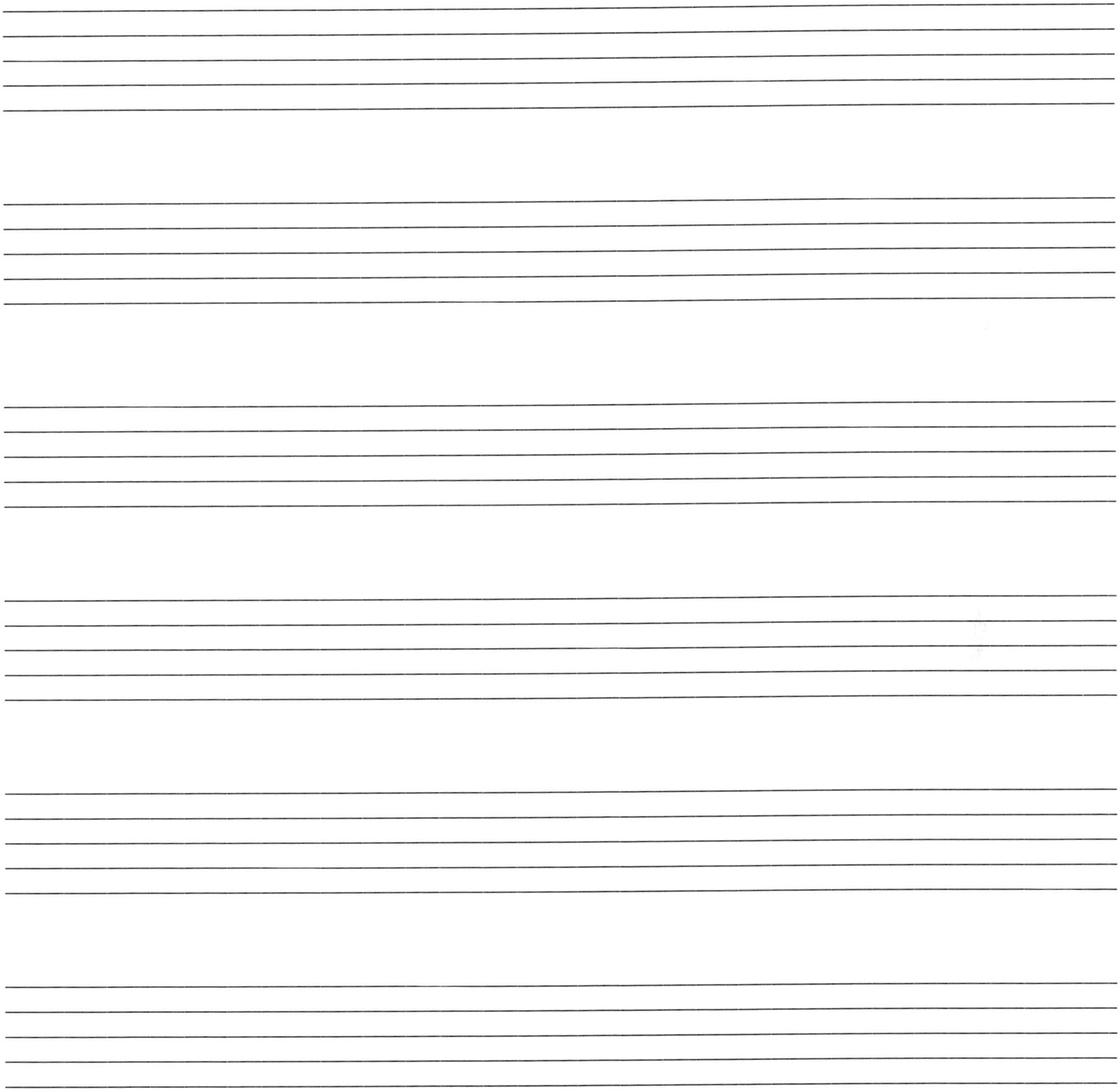

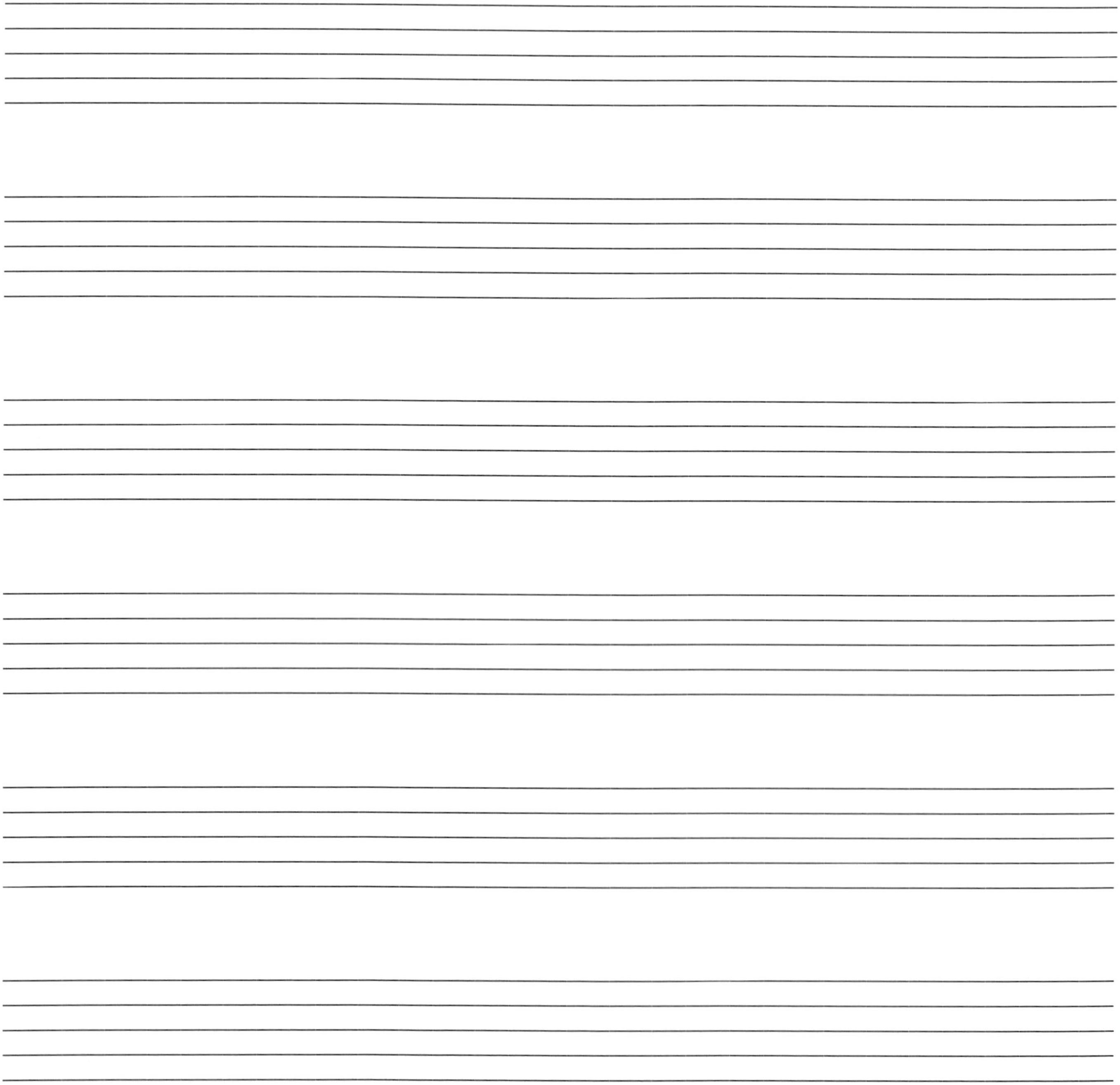

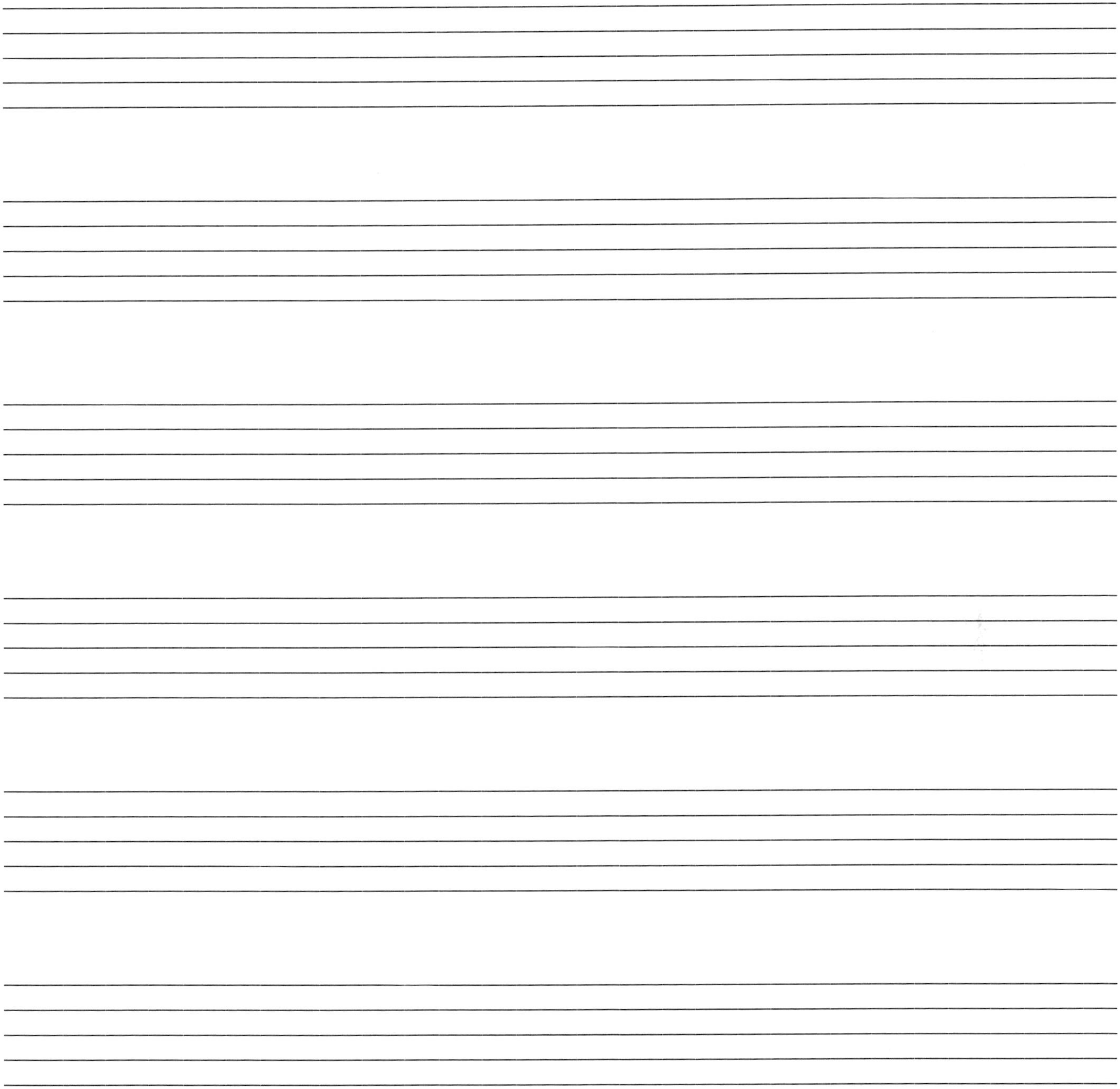

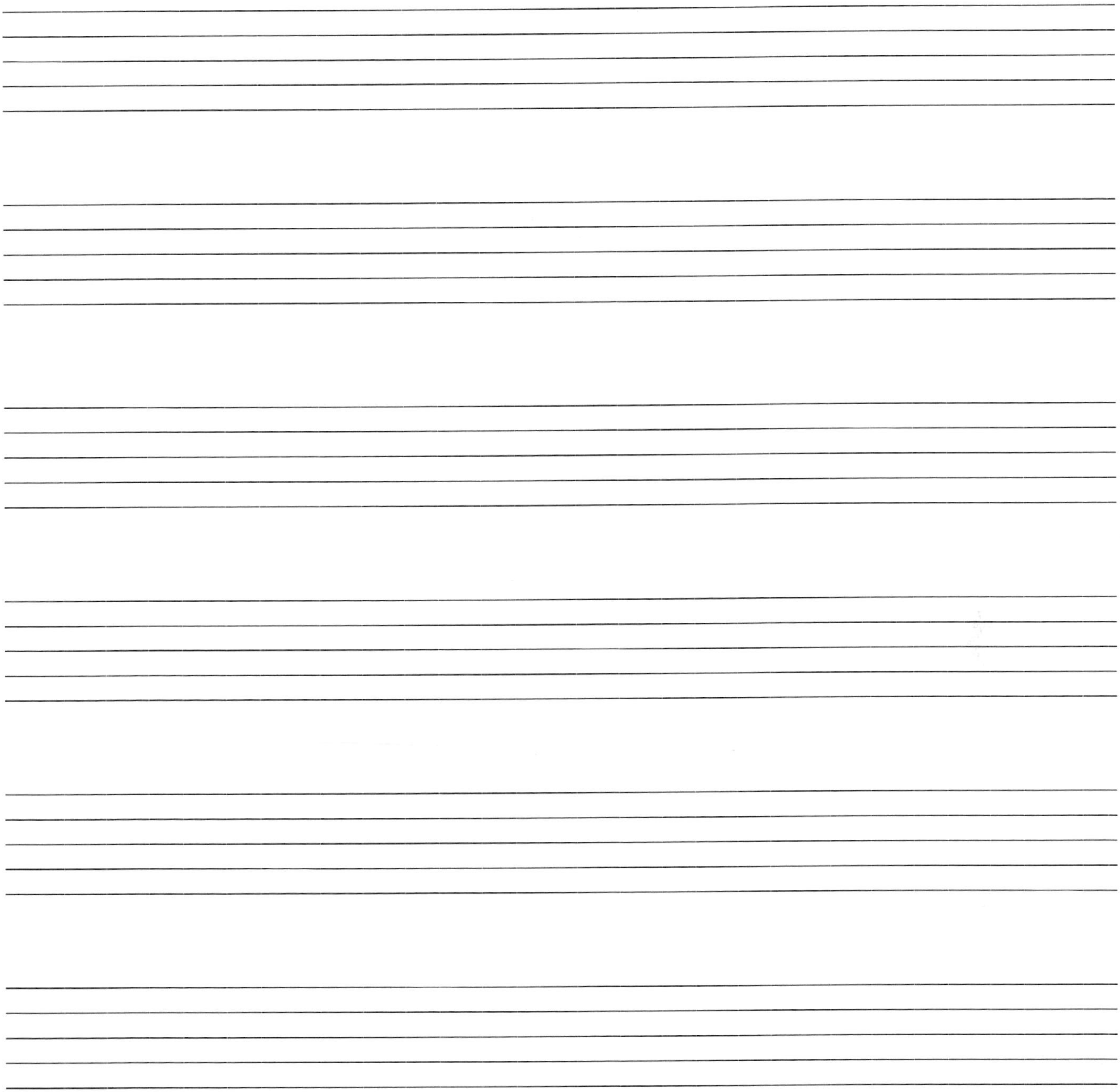

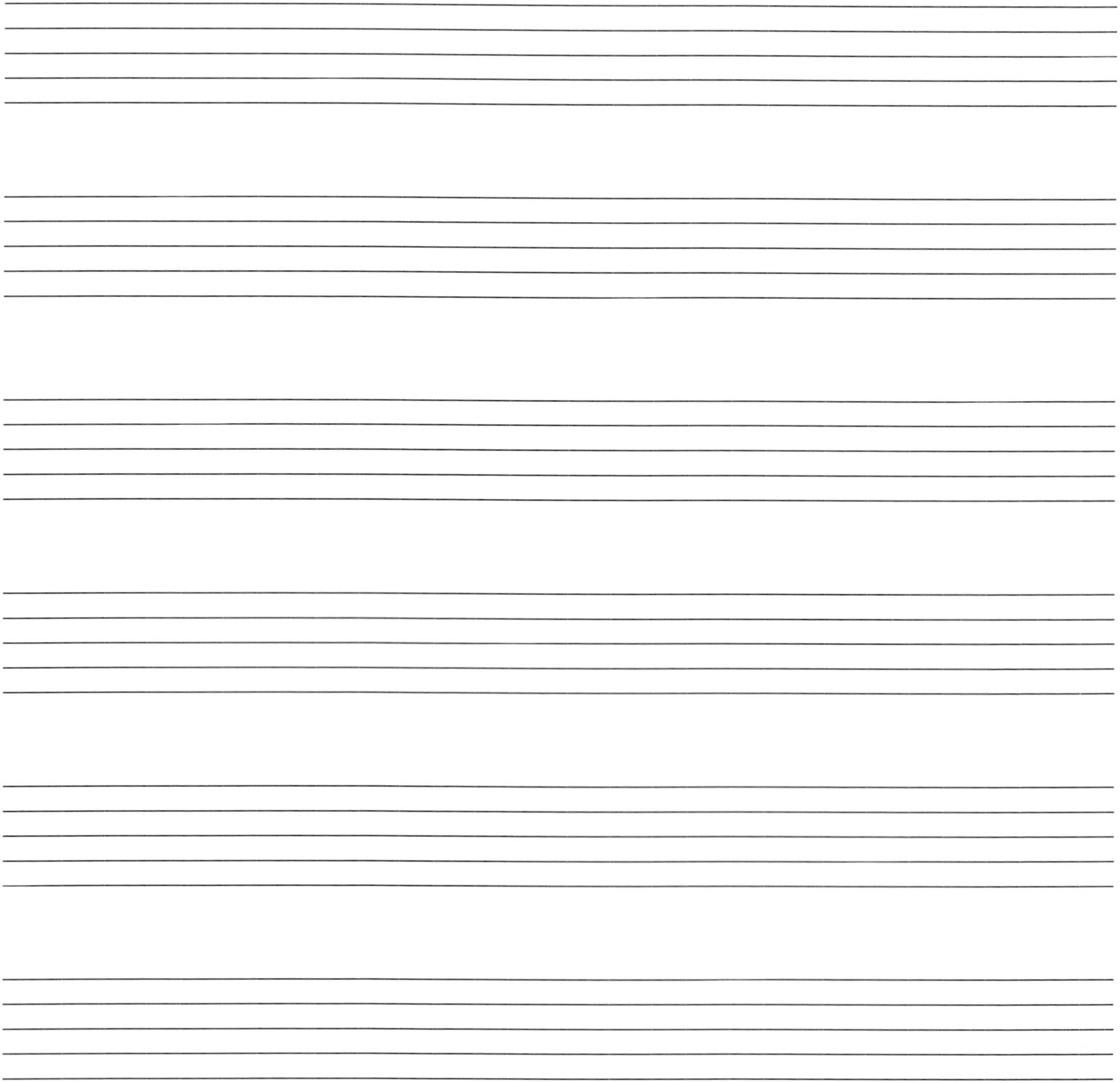

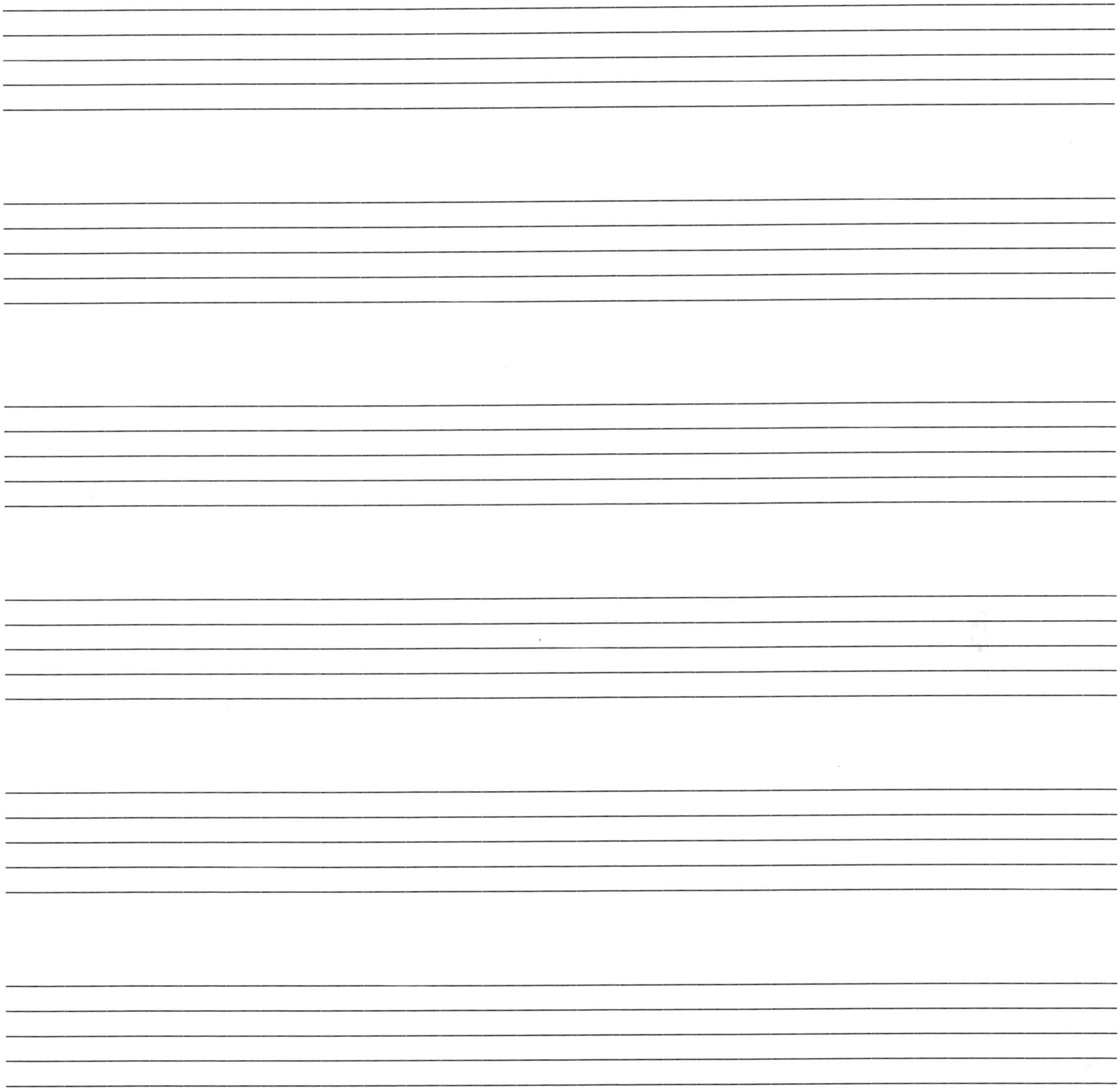

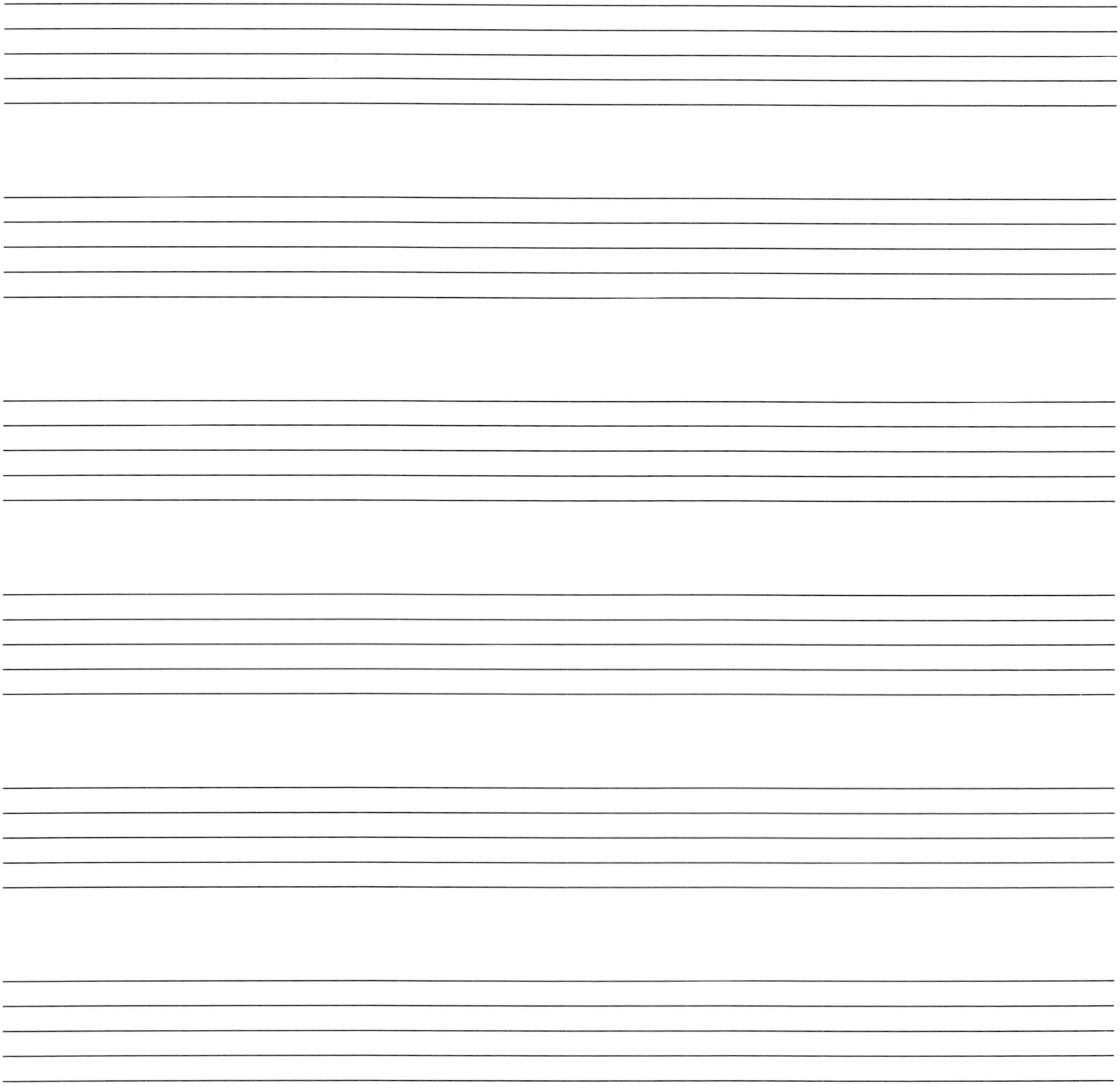

9629205R00022

Printed in Great Britain
by Amazon.co.uk, Ltd.,
Marston Gate.